The Any Time, Any Place Craft Book

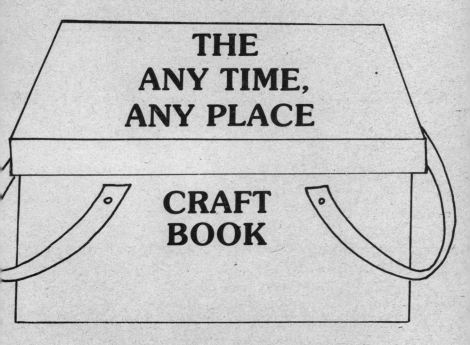

THE
ANY TIME,
ANY PLACE

CRAFT
BOOK

Written and Illustrated by
Roz Abisch and Boche Kaplan

Xerox Education Publications
Middletown, Connecticut

for Helen and Ed Kroop

This book is a presentation of
The Popcorn Bag

Weekly Reader Book Division offers book clubs for
children from preschool to young adulthood. All
quality hardcover books are selected by a distinguished
Weekly Reader Selection Board.

For further information write to:
Weekly Reader Book Division
1250 Fairwood Avenue
Columbus, Ohio 43216

TABLE OF CONTENTS

INTRODUCTION ———————— 7

FUN AND GAMES
Craft Box ———————————— 8
Super Bubble Blower ————— 12
Doodle Board ———————— 14
Carry-Along Checkers ———— 16
Paper-Bag Puppets ————— 18
Bumper Sticker —————— 20

DRESS-UPS
Crazy Glasses ——————— 22
Safe and Sounder ————— 25
Indian Headband ————— 27
Mad-Hatter ——————— 28
String Rings ——————— 31

T-T-T-T-T-SHIRTS
Stylish Stencil T-Shirt ———— 33
Big Initial Stamp —————— 36
Big Initial T-Shirt ————— 40
Tie-Dye T-Shirt —————— 42
Un-Embroidery T-Shirt ——— 44
Do-It-Yourself T-Shirt ——— 46

PERSONAL-ITIES

Three-D Greeting Cards _____ 48

Pet Rock Pets _____ 51

Letter-Getter _____ 52

Hang-Ups _____ 54

Silly Snakes _____ 56

Wall Talkers _____ 57

SHOW-OFFS

Eggshell Mosaic _____ 59

Whirly-Twirly _____ 61

INTRODUCTION

It is great to be able to do something all by your-self. It is great to be able to show your family and friends what you have done. It is great fun to be able to create something special, and there are a lot of special projects for you in this book. Part of what makes the projects so special is that you can work on many of them at almost any time and in almost any place.

CRAFT BOX

Indoors or outdoors,
Alone or with friends,
Holidays or free time,
Vacations or weekends—

Just pack your craft box—
Fill up all the space—
And you're set for fun,
Any time, any place.

To make a CRAFT BOX
you will need:

a large, sturdy cardboard shoe box with a
cover
a pencil
a ruler
scissors
2 strips of cardboard 1″ × 18″
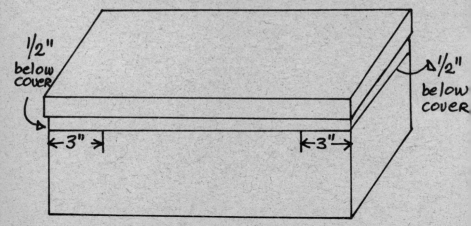
4 paper fasteners
white glue
colored paper or felt

1. Put the cover on the shoe box.

2. With the ruler and the pencil, measure and draw a line ½" below the cover along all four sides of the box. Then remove the cover and set it aside.

3. On the long sides of the box, measure and make a mark on the line 3" in from each corner.

4. Use the tip of the scissors to make a small hole at each 3" mark.

5. Measure and draw a line 1" in from both ends of each 1" × 18" cardboard strip.

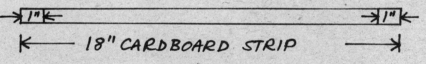

6. Divide and mark the lines in half. At each mark make a small hole with the tip of the scissors.

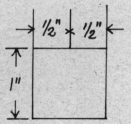

7. Place the ends of a paper fastener first through the hole in one end of a cardboard strip, then through a hole on the outside of the shoe box.

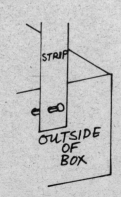

8. Bend the ends of the fastener open on the inside of the box to keep the strip in place.

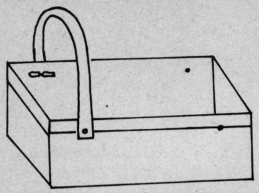

9. Bring the other end of the strip across the top
   of the box and fasten it in the same way.

10. Attach the second cardboard strip to the box
    by following steps 7 through 9.

11. The two cardboard strips will be the handles of
    the box. They can be moved outward to allow
    you to cover and uncover the box.

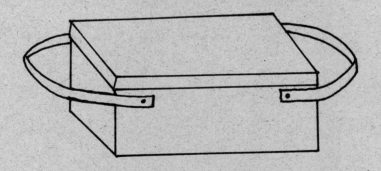

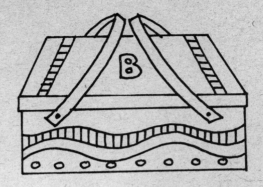

12. They can be moved together toward the center to allow you to carry the box.

13. Use glue and pieces of colored paper and felt to decorate the cover and sides of the box.

14. Save all sorts of small containers. You can use them to store and separate the things you will want to pack in the CRAFT BOX . . . along with your ANY TIME, ANY PLACE CRAFT BOOK.

SUPER BUBBLE BLOWER

You can blow really super bubbles with this super bubble blower.

To make a SUPER BUBBLE BLOWER
you will need:

> the plastic carrying frame from a soft drink six-pack
> a plastic pull-off strip from a frozen juice can
> scissors
> a stapler

1. With the scissors, cut away a double section and a single section from the plastic carrying frame.

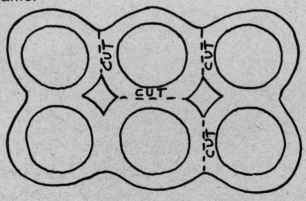

2. Overlap the cut sections and staple them together.

3. Fold the plastic pull-off strip in half.

4. Staple the folded strip to the center of the double section as shown. The strip will make a handle or holding loop for the SUPER BUBBLE BLOWER.

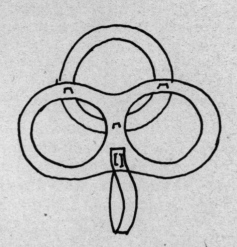

5. Mix equal amounts of liquid soap and water in a medium-size bowl. Hold the loop and swish the bubble blower around in the soap mixture. Then blow through the rings to make bubbles.

DOODLE BOARD

Doodle or draw or tic-tac-toe,
Whenever you want or wherever you go.

To make a DOODLE BOARD
you will need:

> a piece of heavy cardboard 6″ × 9″
> a piece of white paper 6″ × 9″
> white glue
> a piece of plastic wrap 9″ × 12″
> water-soluble felt-tipped markers
> a piece of damp paper towel or a pre-moistened towelette

1. For the front of the doodle board, keep all edges even and glue the white paper to the cardboard.

2. Cover the white paper with the plastic wrap. Bring the plastic around to the back of the cardboard and tape it smoothly in place.

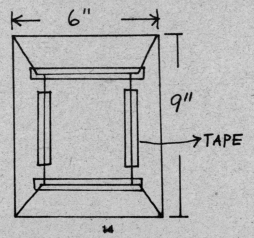

3. Doodle or draw on the front of the board with the water-soluble markers.

4. Wipe the board clean with the damp paper towel or the towelette and you are ready to start all over again.

CARRY-ALONG CHECKERS

This checker set is always on hand when you want to play the game.

To make CARRY-ALONG CHECKERS
you will need:

      a piece of red felt 12″ square
      a ruler
      a permanent-color black fine-point marker
      a permanent-color black felt-tipped marker
      12 flat red buttons ¾″ in diameter
      12 flat black buttons ¾″ in diameter
      2 large blanket safety pins about 3″ long
      and ½″ wide

1. With the ruler and the fine-point marker, measure and draw in a 2″ border along all four sides of the 12″ felt square.

2. Measure and mark each side of the border into 1″ sections.

3. Draw lines connecting the marks from top to bottom and from side to side. You will have 64 1″ squares.

4. Finish the checker board by coloring in every other square with the felt-tipped marker.

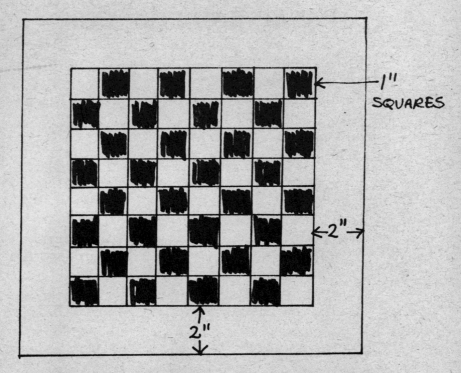

1" SQUARES

2"

2"

5. Slide 12 red buttons onto one safety pin. Slide 12 black buttons onto the other safety pin. Then fasten both pins to the border of the checker board.

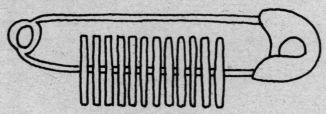

6. Fold the felt board over the pins and buttons and slip your CARRY-ALONG CHECKERS into a pocket.

PAPER-BAG PUPPETS

A brown paper lunch bag can do a lot more than just hold sandwiches. With a little imagination, you can turn it into almost anything you want it to be.

To make a PAPER-BAG PUPPET
you will need:

> a flat-bottom paper lunch bag about 10½"
> long and 5" wide
> a pencil
> felt-tipped markers or crayons in assorted
> colors
> colored construction paper
> colored yarn
> scissors
> white glue

1. With the pencil, draw a face on the flat bottom of the lunch bag.

2. Color in the face and fill in the long part of the bag beneath it with the felt-tipped markers or crayons.

3. Complete the puppet by gluing on pieces of construction paper and yarn. Make hats and buttons, collars and ties with the paper. Use the yarn for hair or whiskers.

4. To make the puppet's head move, open the bag. Slip four fingers into the flat bottom of the bag. Keep your thumb in the long part of the bag. Then move your fingers up and down.

BUMPER STICKER

What's the good word? You can let the whole world know. Just paste a sticker on your bike or wagon, buggy or car.

To make each BUMPER STICKER
you will need:

> a ruler
> a pencil
> a piece of plain paper 9″ × 12″
> a strip of white or light-colored washable adhesive-backed paper 2½″ × 9″
> a permanent-color fine-point marker
> permanent-color felt-tipped markers
> reflective adhesive tape
> scissors

1. Use the ruler, pencil, and paper to plan and design your slogan.

2. Copy the slogan onto the adhesive-backed paper with the fine-point marker. Color it in with the felt-tipped markers. For safety, use pieces of reflective adhesive tape as part of the design.

3. Peel the backing off the paper and paste the BUMPER STICKER in place.

FOR WAGONS, BUGGIES, CARS

2½"

9"

2½"

Super Kid

2½"

2½"

9"

FOR BIKES

CRAZY GLASSES

These sunglasses are sure to catch everyone's eye!

To make CRAZY GLASSES
you will need:

> a piece of cardboard 3″ × 8″
> a pencil
> a ruler
> a compass
> scissors
> 2 pieces of transparent colored celophane
>   or transparent lightweight plastic 2½″
>   square
> white glue
> scraps of colored paper, felt, or trim
> felt-tipped markers
> 2 pieces of string or yarn 9″ long

1. With the ruler and the pencil, measure and mark the 3″ × 8″ piece of cardboard as shown.

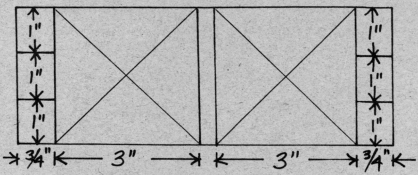

2. Find the center of each 3″ square by drawing diagonal lines from corner to corner.

3. In each square, place the point of the compass where the two lines cross. Make one circle 3″ in diameter. Make another circle 2″ in diameter.

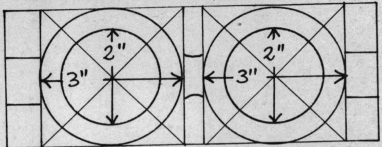

4. Draw two curved lines to connect the 3″ circles in the middle of the board.

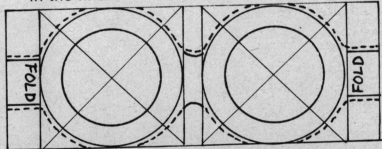

5. Cut the cardboard along the dotted lines with the scissors. DO NOT CUT ON THE FOLD LINES.

6. Trim each 2½″ square of transparent colored cellophane or plastic into the shape of a circle with the scissors.

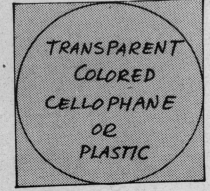

7. Turn the cardboard frame over. Run a thin line of white glue a little in from the edge around each inner circle. Then set a piece of cellophane or plastic over the glue.

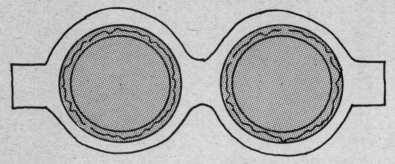

8. When the glue is dry, turn the frame over again. With the point of the compass, make a small hole in the center of each tab at the sides of the frame. Then fold the tabs back at the line.

9. Decorate the glasses with felt-tipped markers. Or glue on scraps of colored paper, felt, or trim.

10. Knot one 9″ piece of string or yarn through the hole in each tab. Use the string or yarn to tie on your CRAZY GLASSES.

SAFE AND SOUNDER

This is an old magic charm that people used to think would keep them safe from harm.

To make a SAFE AND SOUNDER
you will need:

> a piece of heavy cardboard
> self-hardening clay
> a compass and pencil
> a toothpick
> a plastic knife
> yellow and brown paint
> paint brushes
> colorless nail polish
> a piece of narrow ribbon or yarn 18" long

1. On the cardboard, pat and roll out the clay until it is about ¼" thick and 4" in diameter.

2. With the compass, draw six circles on the clay ¼" apart. As you draw, press the pencil into the clay to leave the outline of each circle.

3. Use the point of the compass to outline a tab at the top of the largest circle. Make a hole in the tab with the compass point.

4. Make the outlines of the circles deeper and clearer with the end of the toothpick. Then use the plastic knife to trim away the extra clay as shown by the dotted lines.

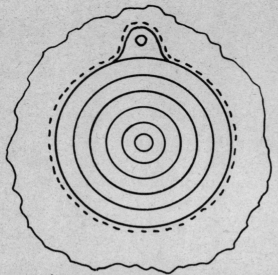

5. After the clay is hard, paint the charm in alter-
    nating rings of yellow and brown.

6. When the paint is dry, coat it with colorless nail
    polish.

7. Loop the ribbon
    or yarn through
    the tab and tie
    your SAFE AND
    SOUNDER around
    your neck.

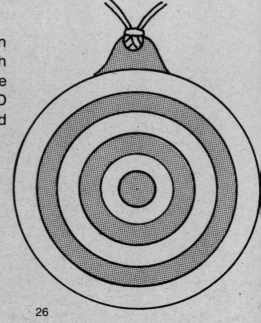

INDIAN HEADBAND

Do you have flyaway hair? Here's a neat way to keep it neat.

To make an INDIAN HEADBAND *you will need:*

> 1 yard (36") of colored ribbon
>   2" wide
> a ruler
> a soft black pencil
> scissors
> scraps of colored felt
> white glue

1. With the ruler and the pencil, measure and draw a line 9" in from each end of the ribbon.

|← 9" →|← 18" →|← 9" →| 18"

2. Use the pencil to draw an Indian design on the 18" section remaining in the middle of the ribbon.

3. With the scissors, cut scraps of felt to fit the shapes in the design.

4. Glue the felt onto the ribbon.

5. Run a thin line of glue along each cut end to keep the ribbon from fraying.

6. Wait until the glue is dry before you tie your INDIAN HEADBAND.

MAD-HATTER

Big hat, tall hat, wide brim or small — the maddest hat is the best hat of all.

To make a MAD-HATTER
you will need:

> several sheets of old newspaper
> 2 large pieces of colored comics 24" square
> 1 large piece of plain paper 24" square
> a small bowl
> water
> a cellulose sponge
> white glue
> a bowl or container that fits over your head
> a large rubber band or a piece of string 24" long
> scissors
> clear spray shellac
> ribbon or trim, felt or feathers

1. Place several sheets of old newspaper on a flat surface. Set one square of colored comics on the newspaper.

2. Put some water in the small bowl.

3. Squeeze white glue onto the comics.

4. Dip the sponge in water. Use the wet sponge to spread the glue evenly all over the comics.

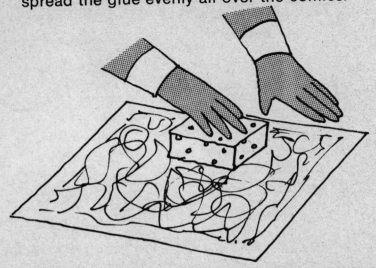

5. Set the square of plain paper over the comics. Try to match up all the edges. Squeeze glue onto the plain paper. Spread the glue with the wet sponge.

6. Cover the plain paper with the second square of comics. Again, try to match up the edges. Run your hands over the papers to press them together into one square.

7. Center the square over the bottom of the bowl or container that fits your head. With your hands, smooth it down over the sides to form the top, or crown, of the hat. Keep the crown of the hat in place with a large rubber band or by tying it with string.

8. The edges of the square that stick out from under the rubber band or string will make the brim of the hat. As the paper dries, bend the brim to the shape you want.

9. When the hat is completely dry, remove the rubber band or string. Lift the hat from the bowl or container. If you wish, round off the edges of the brim with the scissors.

10. To make the hat waterproof, give it several light coats of spray shellac. Allow each coat to dry before you apply the next.

11. Decorate the MAD-HATTER with ribbon or trim, felt or feathers.

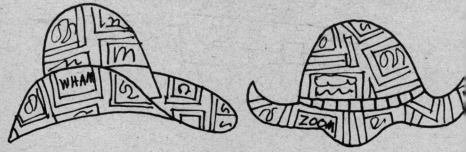

STRING RINGS

Some people tie a string around a finger to keep from being forgetful. But these rings are things you are sure to remember.

To make a STRING RING
you will need:

> a pencil
> a piece of waxed paper 12" square
> tape
> heavy string or twine
> scissors
> white glue
> a piece of scrap paper
> felt-tipped markers or paints and brushes
> small beads, seashells or beach stones
> colorless nail polish

1. With the scissors, cut a piece of string or twine that just fits around your finger.

2. Fold the waxed paper in half, then in half again so that it measures 3" × 12".

3. Wrap the folded waxed paper tightly around the pencil until the paper is about the size of your finger. Check the size with the string.

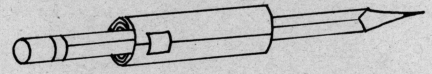

4. Trim away any extra paper with the scissors. Tape the paper together at one end.

5. Wind string or twine around your finger at least three times. The more times it goes around your finger, the wider the ring will be. When you have the width you want, cut the string or twine with the scissors.

6. Squeeze white glue onto the scrap paper. Pull the string or twine through the glue. Be sure it is well coated.

7. Wrap the glue-covered string or twine tightly around the waxed paper on the pencil. Push the rows of string or twine very close together, and press the cut ends into the glue.

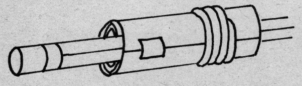

8. Wait until the glue is dry, then gently slide the string or twine off the untaped end of the waxed paper.

9. You can leave the string plain or color it with felt tipped markers or paint.

10. To decorate the ring, glue on small beads, sea-shells or beach stones.

11. Finish the STRING RING by coating it, inside and out, with colorless nail polish.

T - T - T - T - T-SHIRTS

Do you want to wear your own special shirt?
Then make a
STYLISH STENCIL T-SHIRT
or a
BIG INITIAL T-SHIRT
or a
TIE-DYE T-SHIRT
or an
UN-EMBROIDERY T-SHIRT
or a
DO-IT-YOURSELF T-SHIRT!!!

For all but the tie-dye, you will need a white or light-colored cotton T-shirt. Use only a white shirt for the tie-dye. If the shirts are new, wash them first to remove any sizing or finish that may be in the cloth. Before you begin, the shirts should be clean, dry, and smooth. Always wash each completed shirt by hand. For best results, use cold water and a mild liquid detergent.

To make a STYLISH STENCIL T-SHIRT
you will need:

> a piece of cardboard or oaktag 6" × 9"
> a pencil
> scissors or a knife with a sawlike blade
> masking tape
> 3 large grocery bags folded flat
> a deep-colored felt-tipped permanent marker

1. Prepare the stencil by drawing a simple design on the cardboard or oaktag.

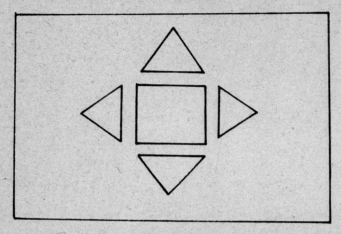

2. Carefully cut out the design with the scissors or the knife.

3. Slide a large grocery bag into the body of the T-shirt. Fold the other two bags to the size of the sleeves and fit them in. The bags will absorb any extra color and keep it from spreading through to the other side of the shirt.

4. Use masking tape to hold the stencil in place on the shirt. Press the stencil flat against the cloth with the fingers of one hand. Color in the cutout areas with a permanent color marker.

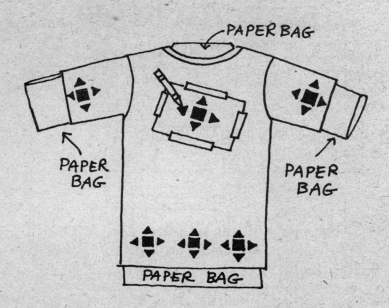

5. Lift the stencil very carefully to keep from smudging the color. Keep placing the stencil on different parts of the shirt until it is printed just the way you want it to be.

6. Try different colors for the shapes on your STYLISH STENCIL T-SHIRT. But remember to let one color dry before you fill in the next one.

BIG INITIAL STAMP

Before you can work on your BIG INITIAL T-SHIRT, you will have to prepare a BIG INITIAL STAMP.

To make a BIG INITIAL STAMP
you will need:

> a pencil
> a ruler
> a piece of tracing paper 1¾" × 3"
> a piece of heavy cardboard 2" × 3¼"
> tape
> scissors
> white glue
> heavy-duty twine
> an empty wooden or plastic thread spool
>   about 1½" high and 1¼" in diameter

1. The initial for the stamp is made out of a double line of heavy-duty twine. For the initial to print clearly, the twine cannot cross or overlap.

2. Here are all the letters of the alphabet, each worked out in a continuous double line. You will have to enlarge them for the stamp.

3. With the ruler and the pencil, measure and draw a 1½″ × 2¾″ rectangle on the tracing paper. Then draw your initial in a dark, double continuous line inside the rectangle.

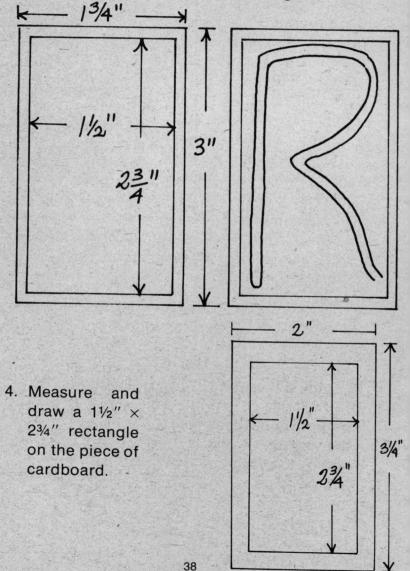

4. Measure and draw a 1½″ × 2¾″ rectangle on the piece of cardboard.

5. Turn the tracing paper over. Match the rectangle on the tracing paper to the one on the cardboard. Tape the paper to the board.

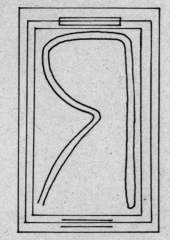

6. With the pencil, go over the lines of your initial that show through the tracing paper. When you remove the paper, your initial will look as if it were written backward on the cardboard.

7. Run a thin line of white glue all around the outlines of your initial. Carefully press the twine into the glue. Use the scissors to trim away the ends of the twine.

8. Allow the glue to dry completely so the twine does not slip. Then turn the cardboard over.

9. Find the center of the cardboard by drawing diagonal lines from corner to corner.

10. Glue the spool over the center of the board to make a handle. Again, allow the glue to dry completely before you use the BIG INITIAL STAMP.

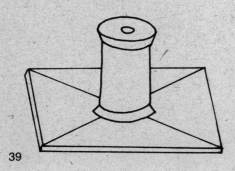

BIG INITIAL T-SHIRT

To make a BIG INITIAL T-SHIRT
you will need:

> 3 large grocery bags folded flat
> a big initial stamp
> a fresh permanent ink stamp pad 2½" × 4"
> or waterproof ink and a shallow dish

1. Slide a large grocery bag into the body of the shirt. Fold the other two bags and fit them into the sleeves.

2. Hold the stamp by the spool. Press it firmly onto the inked surface of the pad. Then print the initial on your shirt. Use only one initial, or continue stamping until the shirt is covered.

3. If you do not have a stamp pad, you can use waterproof ink, instead. Just pour a little ink into a shallow dish. Dip the stamp into the ink, then press it on your BIG INITIAL T-SHIRT.

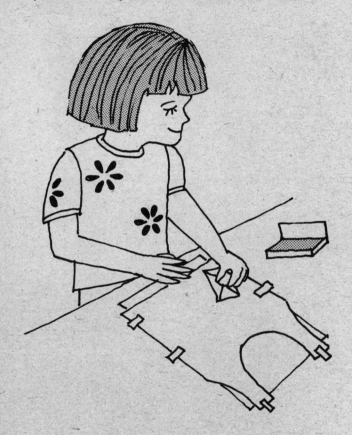

TIE-DYE T-SHIRT

To make a TIE-DYE T-SHIRT
you will need:

> string
> scissors
> an 8-ounce bottle of liquid all-purpose dye
> in a very bright or dark color
> several sheets of old newspaper
> a 4-quart glass bowl or a disposable paint-
> mixing bucket
> a long metal spoon.

1. In order to tie-dye, you have to work with a single layer of cloth. The front and back of the shirt and the front and back of each sleeve have to be tied separately.

2. One section at a time, twist a small part of the cloth into a lump. At the twist, tie the lump tightly with string.

3. Continue to twist and tie until the entire shirt is done. The smaller the lumps, the smaller the design will be.

4. Fill the bowl or bucket three-quarters of the way with warm tap water. The warmer the better, but be sure that the water is not too hot.

5. Place the bowl or bucket on several layers of old newspaper.

6. Add the liquid dye to the water. With the spoon, stir the dye until it is completely blended into the water.

7. Wet the tied shirt in clean water. Squeeze out the excess water, and place the shirt in the dye mixture. The whole shirt should be covered with the dye.

8. Allow the shirt to soak in the dye for at least 30 minutes. The longer it soaks, the darker the color will get.

9. Use the spoon to stir the shirt around in the dye until it is a shade darker than you want it to be.

10. When you are satisfied with the color, lift the shirt out of the dye. Squeeze the excess liquid into the bowl or bucket. Then allow the shirt to dry.

11. When the shirt is completely dry, carefully snip away the strings with the scissors. The parts that were held tightly with the string will be white. The rest of the cloth will be colored.

12. Rinse the shirt in cold water until the water looks clear. After it is dry again, your TIE-DYE T-SHIRT will be ready to wear.

43

UN-EMBROIDERY T-SHIRT

To make an UN-EMBROIDERY T-SHIRT you will need:

>   masking tape
>   a soft black pencil
>   a large grocery bag folded flat
>   fine-point permanent markers in assorted
>   colors

1. Place the shirt on a flat surface. Tape it down to stretch it flat and keep it from slipping. Leave the bottom of the shirt untaped.

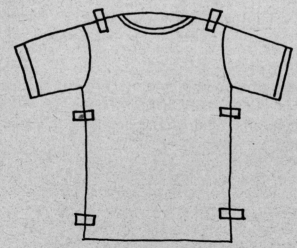

2. With the soft black pencil, lightly draw an embroidery-like design on the front of the shirt.

3. Slip the paper bag into the shirt from the bottom. Set the bag in place under the design.

4. Make the tiny "stitches" in the design with the fine-point markers. Use different colors for different sections.

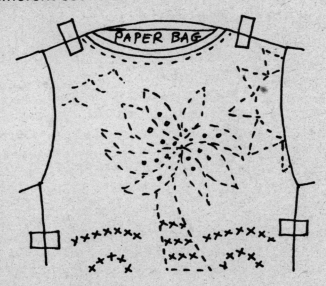

5. Wait until all the colors are dry. Then wash your UN-EMBROIDERY T-SHIRT with cold water and a mild liquid detergent to remove the pencil marks.

DO-IT-YOURSELF T-SHIRT

To make a DO-IT-YOURSELF T-SHIRT
you will need:

> a white, light-colored, or tie-dyed T-shirt
> a soft black pencil
> a piece of white paper 9″ × 12″
> a black fine-point marker
> a large grocery bag folded flat
> felt-tipped permanent markers in assorted
> colors

1. Use the pencil and the paper to plan the design for your shirt.

2. Go over all the pencil lines with the fine-point black marker.

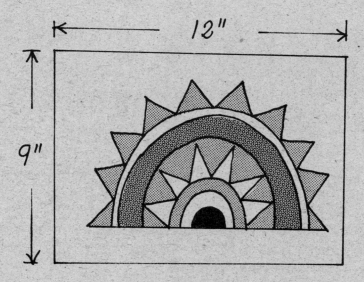

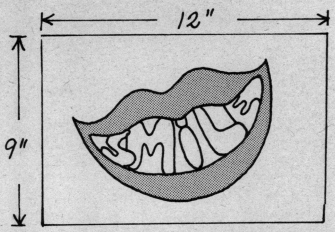

12"

9"

3. Stretch the shirt out on a flat surface. Tape it in place, leaving the bottom open.

4. Slip the paper with the design inside the shirt. Place the design where you want it to be. You will be able to see the black lines through the cloth.

5. Trace the lines of the design onto the shirt with the pencil. Then remove the paper.

6. Slide the grocery bag into the shirt. Be sure it is under the whole design.

7. Color in the design with the permanent markers. Allow one color to dry before you use another.

8. If you like, you can put one design on the front and a different design on the back of your DO-IT-YOURSELF T-SHIRT.

THREE-D GREETING CARDS

Mother's Day, Father's Day, birthdays—whatever. Folks will think that these cards are really quite clever.

To make each THREE-D GREETING CARD *you will need:*

> a plain index card 5" × 8"
> a soft black pencil
> a ruler
> a piece of tracing paper 5" × 8"
> masking tape
> scissors
> white glue
> scraps of colored paper, felt, fabric, yarn, or trim
> fine-point markers

1. Set the tracing paper over the diagram. Tape down the corners.

2. With the ruler and the pencil, trace all the lines onto the paper.

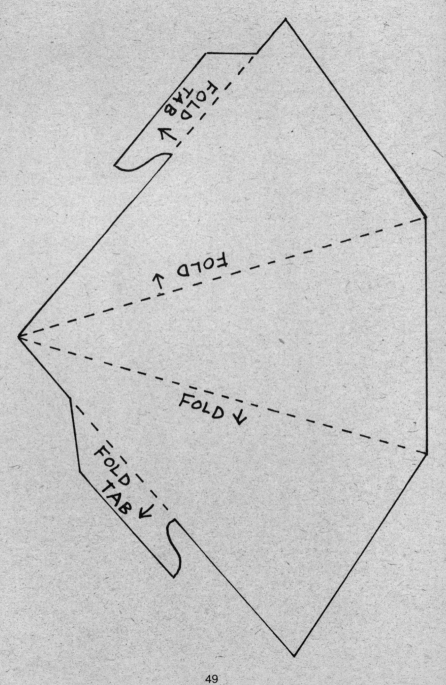

3. Remove the tape and the tracing paper. Turn the tracing paper over. Blacken over all the lines with the side of the pencil point.

4. Turn the tracing paper over again and tape it to the index card. With the ruler and the pencil, trace over all the lines again. When you remove the tracing paper, the lines will be on the card.

5. With the scissors, cut along all the solid lines. Then fold along all the dotted lines.

6. Lay the card flat again. Decorate all three sections. Glue on scraps of colored paper, felt, fabric, yarn, or trim. Write in the greeting you want to use with the markers.

7. Fold the card and lock the tabs as shown.

8. Your THREE-D GREETING CARD will stand on any flat surface.

PET ROCK PETS

These are the best of pets. They don't have to be fed. They don't have to be walked. They don't take up much room. But they are always there when you want to play with them.

To make each PET ROCK PET
you will need:

>   several smooth clean rocks in different shapes and sizes
>   contact glue or epoxy cement
>   felt-tipped markers in assorted colors or paints and brushes
>   colorless nail polish

1. For the body of your pet, choose a rock that fits into the palm of your hand. Sometimes the shape of the rock can help you decide what kind of animal to make.

2. Use smaller rocks to make the other parts of the animal. Attach each small rock to the large one with contact glue or epoxy cement. Hold one rock in place until the glue or cement is dry. Then add the next one.

3. After all the parts are glued in place, decorate your pet with felt-tipped markers or paint. Leave some sections of the rocks plain.

4. To protect the decorations and to bring out the natural color of the stone, coat your PET ROCK PETS with colorless nail polish.

LETTER-GETTER

This is a better letter-getter. It is so much better that you will probably be asked to make more than one.

To make a LETTER-GETTER *you will need:*

> white or light-colored oaktag 4" × 12"
> a ruler
> a pencil
> felt-tipped markers in assorted colors
> scissors
> white glue

1. Use the ruler and the pencil to measure and mark the oaktag to the dimensions shown.

2. With the pencil, draw the shapes of the mail boxes. Color them in with the markers.

3. Cut away the curved sections along the dotted lines with the scissors.

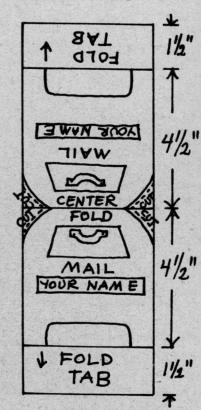

4. Fold the decorated board in half at the center so that there will be a mail box facing out on each side.

5. Fold the bottom tabs under and paste them together with white glue. Allow the glue to dry.

6. Ask your family to place your personal mail in your LETTER-GETTER.

HANG-UPS

Here are hang-ups you won't mind having!

To make each HANG-UP
you will need:

> 1 piece of heavy cardboard or corrugated
> cardboard 12" × 16"
> a ruler
> a pencil
> scissors or a knife with a sawlike blade
> adhesive-backed paper or felt-tipped
> markers in assorted colors
> clear spray shellac

1. With the pencil and the ruler, divide and mark
   the cardboard into 1" squares. In the illustra-
   tion ¼" = 1".

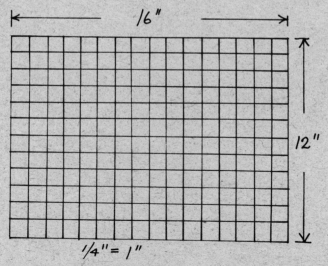

16"

12"

¼" = 1"

2. Following the lines from square to square, trace the shape that is shown onto the piece of cardboard with the pencil.

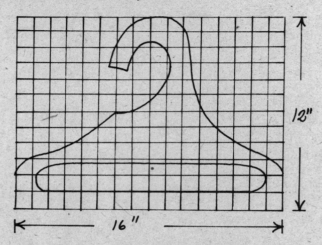

12"

16"

3. Carefully cut out the shape with the scissors or a knife with a saw-like blade.

4. Decorate both sides of the shape with adhesive-backed paper or felt-tipped markers.

5. If you use markers, add a protective finish by spraying on several light coats of clear shellac. Allow each coat of shellac to dry before you apply the next one. Then hang up your HANG-UP.

SILLY SNAKES

You'll never see snakes like these in a zoo. What they end up looking like depends upon you.

To make each SILLY SNAKE
you will need:

> a tie that Dad no longer wants
> scissors; a ruler
> pieces of clean rags or old nylon stockings
> a needle; thread
> scraps of colored felt or paper
> white glue or rubber cement

1. Use the scissors to cut open the stitching at the narrow end of the tie.

2. Push clean rags or old nylons into the tie through the opening. Use the ruler to help stuff the tie all the way down to the wide part.

3. After the tie is stuffed, sew up the opening with the needle and thread.

4. Make eyes, a nose, a mouth, or a tongue out of colored felt or paper. Paste them on the wide end of the tie with white glue or rubber cement. Try to see how silly you can make your SILLY SNAKE look.

WALL TALKERS

If the walls could talk, what would they say? Here's a chance to say it your way.

To make a WALL TALKER
you will need:

> a piece of bright or light-colored felt 9″ × 18″
> a piece of heavy cardboard 1″ × 9″
> a piece of heavy cardboard 1″ × 11″
> scissors
> pieces of dark-colored felt
> white glue
> trim
> yarn

1. Place the 9″ × 18″ piece of felt on a flat surface.

2. With the white glue, paste the 1″ × 9″ cardboard to the felt at the bottom.

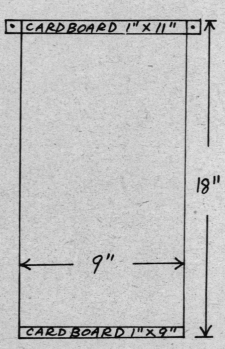

3. Paste the 1″ × 11″ piece of cardboard even with the top of the felt. Allow 1″ of the cardboard to stick out on each side. When the glue is dry, make a hole in each 1″ section of cardboard with the tip of the scissors. Then turn the felt over.

4. Use the scissors to cut the letters for the words of your message out of dark-colored felt.

5. Paste the words in place with white glue.

6. Knot the yarn through the holes in the cardboard at the top of the felt. Use the yarn to hang up the WALL TALKER.

EGGSHELL MOSAIC

This is one way to show that an egg is more than it is cracked up to be.

To make an EGGSHELL MOSAIC
you will need:

>a pencil
>a piece of heavy cardboard
>eggshells
>food coloring in assorted colors
>several small screw-cap jars
>paper towels
>several sheets of old newspaper
>a spoon
>white glue·

1. With the pencil, draw a simple picture or design on the cardboard. Don't make any of the areas too small.

2. Save the shells from eggs used in cooking. The larger your picture or design is, the more shells you will need.

3. Decide on the colors you want to use for your picture or design.

4. For each color you choose, fill a small jar half-way with water. Mix food coloring with the water until you get a rich, dark shade of the color you plan to use.

5. Break the eggshells into small pieces. Add the broken eggshells to the colored water in each of the jars.

6. Screw the caps on the jars and let the eggshells soak. As the shells soak, they will absorb the color. The longer they soak, the darker the color will be.

7. When the eggshells are the color you want, remove them from the jars with a spoon. Spread the shells to dry on several sheets of old newspaper.

8. On your picture or design, apply white glue to one color area at a time. Fit the eggshell pieces into the area as close together as possible.

9. When one section is filled, go on to another. Continue until all the areas are filled and your EGGSHELL MOSAIC is completed.

WHIRLY-TWIRLY

Hang this near a window. It will whirl and twirl in the breeze and shimmer in the light.

To make a WHIRLY-TWIRLY
you will need:

> a piece of colored oaktag 4½" square
> a pencil
> a ruler
> a compass
> scissors
> 12 pieces of medium-weight transparent colored plastic 1" square
> a needle and thread
> colored yarn or twine

1. To find the center of the oaktag square, draw diagonal lines from corner to corner with the pencil and the ruler.

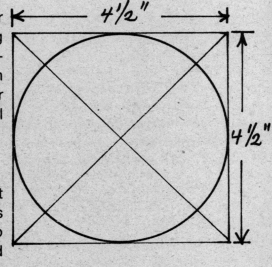

2. Place the point of the compass where the two line cross and draw a circle 4½" in diameter.

3. Use the pencil to draw a continuous spiral line inside the circle.

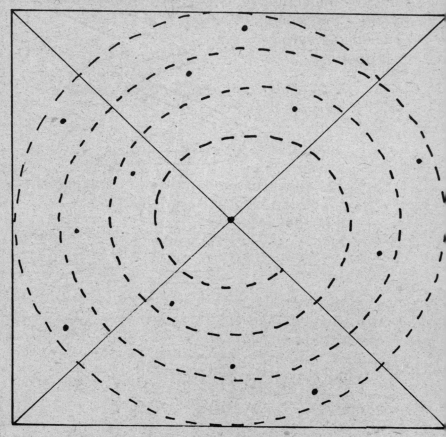

4. Make dots inside the spiral as shown.

5. Carefully make a hole through each dot with the point of the compass.

6. Use the scissors to cut around the circle and along the line of the spiral.

7. Hold the cut oak-
   tag by the center
   and the end.
   Then gently pull
   it open.

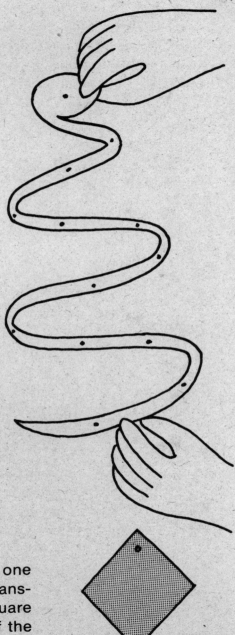

8. Make a hole in one
   corner of each trans-
   parent plastic square
   with the point of the
   needle.

9. Use the needle and thread to knot and attach a plastic square to each hole in the oaktag except the one in the center.

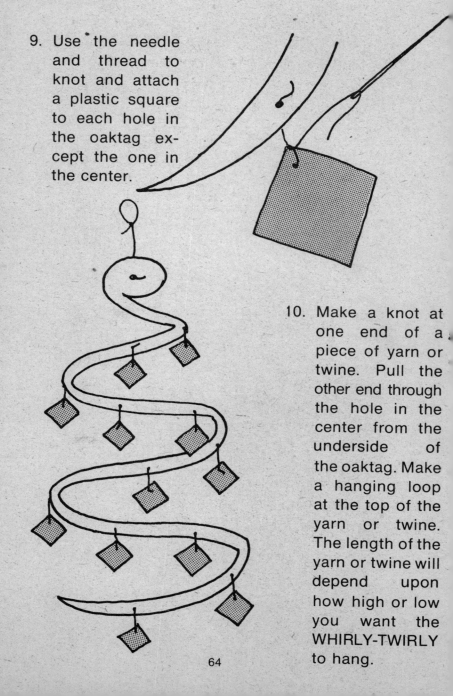

10. Make a knot at one end of a piece of yarn or twine. Pull the other end through the hole in the center from the underside of the oaktag. Make a hanging loop at the top of the yarn or twine. The length of the yarn or twine will depend upon how high or low you want the WHIRLY-TWIRLY to hang.